With Raspberry Tea

E.E. Sorrells

Illustrated by Alexis Goar

With Raspberry Tea

Copyright © 2020 by Eryn Sorrells

All rights reserved.

Library of Congress Control Number: 2020925617

ISBN: 978-1-7363658-0-9 (paperback)

ISBN: 978-1-7363658-1-6 (e-book)

Written by E.E. Sorrells

Illustrated by Alexis Goar

First printing 2021

For the people who supported me,

Through all my life.

And

For all my readers,

For making my dreams come true.

Table of Contents

FALL 1

    FALL 2
    PAPER SKIN 3
    WRITERS BLOCK 4
    LOVE OR LOST 5
    BROKEN 6
    HOLLOW 7
    NEVER LOVED 8
    HAIR 9
    EMPTY 10
    SOMEONE ELSE'S 11
    NEVER 12
    SILENCE, SOUND, AND YOU 13
    COOL CITY FALLS 14
    BROKEN PROMISES 15
    AFRAID 16
    NOBODY KNOWS 17
    SONGBIRD 18
    HISTORY 19
    IN MY MIND 20
    MEMORIES 21
    SHATTERED SCREEN 22
    I AM 23
    PRETTY COLORS 24
    A LYING MIND 25
    SILENCE 26
    PERMANENT 27
    HEALING 28
    COLD HEART 29
    BREAKING 30
    CINNAMON 31
    MOTHS 32
    AGING 33

MIND VS EYES	34
CHANGE	35
CRUEL	36
LITTLE PINK TONGUE	37
TEARFUL BUTTERFLIES	38
THE BROKEN HEARTED	39
MASQUERADE	40
SKY	41
HARMFUL WORDS	42
CHURCH BELLS	43
THOSE WHO CAN'T COUNT	44
WHAT	45
A SILENCE ANSWERED	46
NO FIGHT	47
ONE-SIDED	48
SLEEP	49
MY BODY	50
FOR SOMEONE LIKE YOU	51
A HOLE IN MY SHOE	52
JEALOUSY	53
DEBT	54
STRESS	55
TRAGEDY	56
MIND GAMES	57
ENVY	58
NO FIGHT LEFT	59
THE FLOOR	60
DEAR FLOWERS	61
KINDNESS	62
WAITING	63
VOLCANO	64
LIES	65
MY HAIR	66
ICE	67
WHY	68
TEARS	69
STATISTIC	70
WINTER	**71**
WINTER	72
WITH RASPBERRY TEA	73

WISHING FOR MORE	74
HURT	75
STAPLES	76
HIM	77
BLADED TONGUE	78
A TOAST TO HARSH WORDS	79
A EULOGY FOR MY HEART AND MIND	80
TOYS	81
NOTHING	82
A LOVE LETTER TO THE VOICES IN MY HEAD	83
MY VOICE	84
SNOWFLAKES	85
FROSTBITE	86
HERE WE ARE	87
CROSS	88
MEAN	89
HATE	90
IF SIZE MATTERED	91
DEATH	92
LAND AND SEA	93
SINS	94
DAY 1	95
REAL PAIN	96
REALIZATION	97
BLOOD	98
LINES FROM A SHATTERED SOUL	99
YOUTH	100
WRITING	101
LYING	102
I IMAGINE	103
CRYING PHONE	104
PAIN AND LOVE	105
TO A BROKEN HEART	106
ACTION'S VOICE	107
LOOK AT ME	108
UNPAVED	109
I SIT	110
AWAY FROM ME	111
INSANITY	112
TALKING TO THE WORLD	113
RELAPSE	114

- INSIDE AND OUT ... 115
- STILL LOVE ME ... 116
- HEALING CAN HURT ... 117
- MY MIND ... 118
- WITHOUT YOU ... 119
- PUSH ME DOWN ... 120
- MUSIC ... 121
- ATTACHMENT ... 122
- MY DEAR ... 123
- WITH THE EFFORT OF MOVING ... 124
- LETTERS ... 125
- VIOLENCE ... 126
- CYANIDE ... 127
- DENIAL ... 128
- REPEAT ... 129
- AN ANGEL'S KISS ... 130
- PAIN THAT LOVES ME ... 131
- HOW COULD YOU ... 132
- THE SILENT BLADE ... 133
- BIRDS ... 134
- A KISS ... 135
- LOVE SCAR ... 136
- LOST ... 137
- ANXIETY ... 138
- DEAD BUTTERFLIES ... 139
- ROPE ... 140
- MUCH TOO WELL ... 141
- COMPLIMENTS ... 142
- MY FOE ... 143
- THE MOON ... 144
- SHARP BLADE ... 146
- DEATH DOESN'T SEEM ... 147
- A STABBING ... 148
- BEFORE OR AFTER ... 149

SPRING ... 150

- SPRING ... 151
- I DREAM IN BRIGHT COLORS ... 152
- RASPBERRY ... 153
- LAVENDER ... 154
- FIRE ... 155

INCOMPLETE	156
YOUR WORTH	157
LOVE	158
YOU FIRST	159
SCIENTIST	160
HOLEY	161
IF YOU LOVE	162
MUSICAL DREAMS	163
I DREAM	164
I CAN WRITE OUT MY OWN FUTURE	165
FAKE SMILES	166
YOUR EYES	167
SNOW	168
LET HER GROW	169
CARDINAL	170
QUESTIONS	171
SUNSHINE	172
CATS	173
A BEAUTIFUL MIND	174
WORDS	175
ADDICTION	176
FEAR OF GROWTH	178
MY HEART	179
IF MY SCARS COULD TALK	180
ROUGHLY	181
PASTELS	182
MY WRITING	184
FOREST OF MY SCALP	185
MY LITTLE FLOWER	186
CURRENCY OF LOVE	187
LOVING MYSELF	188
YOUR KISS	189
THE DIFFERENCE	190
DO FLOWERS BLOOM?	191
WHAT'S WRONG WITH LOVING YOU?	192
THE MEADOW	193
DO I KNOW LOVE?	194
WHOEVER YOU WANT	195
BEAUTIFUL	196
I'M HUNGRY FOR YOU	197
I ONLY HAVE HORNS	198

THE RAIN	199
SHARP EDGES	200
DO YOU LOVE ME?	201
MOON LOVER	202
HER SMILE	203
WHAT IF I WERE THE MOON?	204
POTHOLES	206
BUTTERFLY	207
I LOVE ME	208

SUMMER **209**

SUMMER	210
WE ARE ALL PEOPLE	211
EVERYWAY	212
DEAR GIRL	213
MY HOME	214
COUNTRY SUMMERS	215
PRECIOUS CHILD	216
TAP YOUR FOOT	217
OPAL	218
LATE NIGHT WRITING	219
THE DARK	220
MIDNIGHT	221
ODE TO THE VOICE	222
TOUCH A STAR	223
COLORBLIND	224
WHAT IS BEAUTIFUL	225
I DON'T CARE	226
YOU	227
LOVE	228
SKELETON	229
THE HEART RING	230
YOUR AFFECTION	231
SHOWERS	232
A POEM	233
TO THE READER	234
SWEET	235
BE TRUE	236
PAINTING	237
I AM A WOMAN	238
THE SKY	241

Who I Am 242
Commander 243
The Cup 244

Fall

Fall

The leafless trees,
They wave to me in the wind,
Like an old friend wishing me away.

The birds in the branches,
Like dark eyes,
Wink to me as I pass.

The cool winds,
Like soft whispers,
Speak to me as I prance.

The dead leaves,
Like flakey puff pastry,
Crumble beneath me.

The sweet fall,
Like a welcome to winter,
Drifts around me.

Paper Skin

Like a dull pencil
Carving into me.
You wrote out your pain.
Never thinking
Of the paper beneath you.

Writers Block

Writer's block
is not a loss for words,
But a loss for feelings.

Love or Lost

When that chill
runs down your body
You either loved or lost.
The pain of both can dance down you.

Broken

The whispers behind you,
Are not always about you.
Stop thinking they are.
Don't let others break you,
You've broken yourself enough.

Hollow

The hollow feeling you are becoming,
It will not be permanent.
Do not let it consume who you were,
or who you are.

Never Loved

As time passes,
I've learned to understand,
You may love him,
But he never loved you.

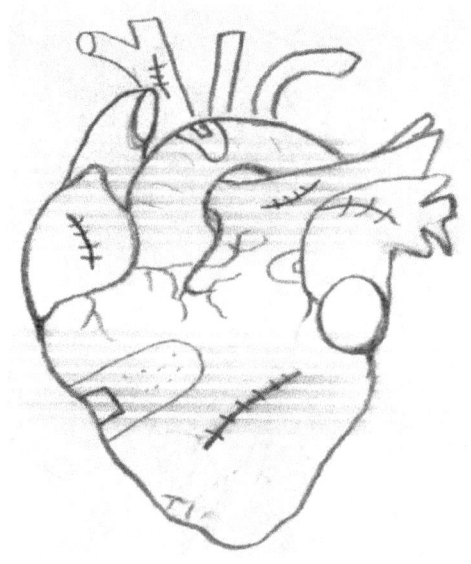

Hair

The colors of the leaves change, like the color of our hair. They go from vibrant hues to gorgeous shades of red. Unlike the leaves, we try to alter our beauty. Hiding the snow shade hairs that we earned by living.

Empty

Do not love the empty feeling in your stomach.
It can feel like heaven and hurt like hell,
but it will not leave you on Earth.

Someone Else's

If they make you wonder if they care.
If they make you beg for attention.
If they make you think you aren't enough,
They are not yours,
They are someone else's.

Never

The scar on your mind may never be healed.
The scratches on your body may never be gone.
The tears in your eyes may never fall.
The hole on your heart may never be filled.*

*you just have to live

Silence, Sound, and You

Silence may be your best friend.
Silence may be your worst enemy.
Sound may be your best friend.
Sound may be your worst enemy.
You may be your best friend.
But never be your worst enemy.

Cool City Falls

A crisp fall Dawn
And a cool fall dusk.
The smooth paint brush strokes of the sun.
The city lights glow out
Like the lightning bugs of the summer.
The fallen leaves—
Dancing in my path—
Seem to lure me forward.
I follow the wind,
Letting it lead me home
To my cool city falls.

Broken Promises

Like an echo to all.
The promise of a longer life.
The promise of a brighter smile.
The promise of a peppier step.
The promise of a relaxed love.
The promise of a new self.

Let my promise ring,
Like an echo to all,
With my fingers crossed behind me.

Afraid

In the ocean
I'll never be.
As I am afraid of what's in it.
The dark depths that surround the world
Hold more mysteries unknown.
I fear the ocean,
And what confides in its dark crystal waves.

In my imagination I live,
For
In the world
I'll never be,
As I am afraid of what's in it.

Nobody Knows

The chills down your back
—Like the mountains in the south—
Rise and fall with time.
The cool winds bite at them,
While you pass down the road.
Nobody knows what the cool wind can tell you,
No body but the Mountains.

Songbird

I tried to sing for you,
Like a songbird in a choir,
Just outside your window.
You must have hated bird songs,
As you chose to shut the glass.

History

Our history was made.
Full of wars,
of peace,
Full of love,
of death.
I wish we were doomed,
Doomed to repeat every second

In My Mind

I would sit there and write.
I would write anything that came to mind.
Poems about pain.
About love.
About loss.
About joy.
But every time, I thought about you.

Memories

Don't let their memory love you.
Don't let your dream of them love you.
If they don't love,
They don't love.
Don't make yourself sit through the torture of imagined love,
It will hurt worse than a knife ever will.

Shattered Screen

The screen of my phone flickered,
Much like the old soul within me.
It followed my heartbeat.
Flashing at the tempo it set.

I replaced my phone.

If I could only do that for a broken soul.*

*a broken phone

I am

I am an empty shell,
A cicada after the first months of life.

I am a ghost,
A spirit after the love I had in life.

I am a tension in the room,
An uncomfortable silence between two beautiful people.

I am a shadow in the day,
Something so forgettable no one cares.

I am a moth in the night,
never mistaken for a butterfly again.

Pretty Colors

I wish I could paint myself,
The way I paint my nails.
The pretty colors distract
From what is broken and dirty.
The colors make them look beautiful.

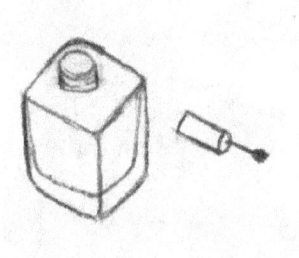

A Lying Mind

Have I ever
felt real pain
Or
Was my mind lying
to me all these years.

Silence

Nothing speaks
louder than
silence in
a noisy
room

Permanent

I rubbed my arm uncomfortably.
He smiled at me and joked.
I want to forget what happened,
But I just can't.
It's like the scars on my arm,
It is permanent.

Healing

How many pages is a book,
I asked the world.
As many as it takes to heal,
She said,
stroking my hair

Cold Heart

Small mistakes
Do not make
you a failure,
Only a cold heart does

Breaking

The tears
that come with healing
Will feel
more like breaking again

Cinnamon

I thought you were sweet
like sugar and cinnamon
But you were as hard to swallow
as cinnamon itself

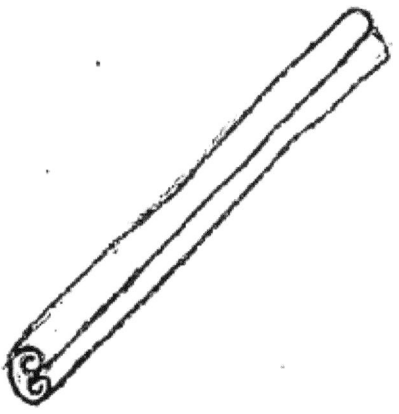

Moths

I was a butterfly,
Mistaken for a moth.
Now I believe that
I am nothing more
Than the creature in the dark.

Aging

What if aging,
Is a magician,
Begging for us to applaud him
As he performs his favorite trick.

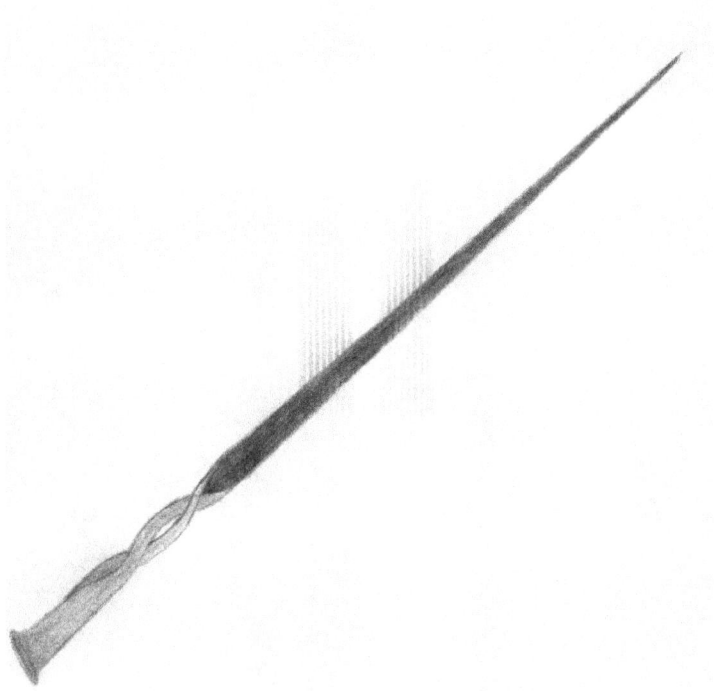

Mind vs Eyes

Is my life as it is in my eyes
Or
As it is in my mind

Change

When do emotions stop being
Love
And start being hate.

When do emotions stop being
Happy
And start being hurt.

When do emotions change
Us?

Cruel

My opinions
Mean nothing to
a cruel world,
Full of cruel people,
With cruel emotions,
Full of cruel pasts,
With cruel pains.

Cruel lives
With nothing but pains,
They hurt the innocence
we all try to hold to.
Such innocence that no longer exists.

Little Pink Tongue

I open my mouth,
Soft opinions on the very tip
Of that little pink tongue.

They make me bite it.

It cuts the opinions off,
Before they had a chance to learn to fly.

Such a thought
—My mind learning to fly—
No pain from a bit tongue.

No blood
Spilling from my lips
As I try to swallow what
Thoughts I have left.

I drown on the scarlet words,
Maybe for the best.

Because I have my opinions
On the tip
Of a little pink tongue.

Tearful Butterflies

The tears in my eyes are
Like the butterflies in my stomach.
The flutter around,
Uncomfortably at best

The Broken Hearted

For the broken hearted:
    Those who lost their dreams,
Those who never started,
    The first ones to leave.
For the ones who died young:
    Those who lost their minds,
Those without words,
    The ones we never find.
For those who want to die:
    Those who wonder,
Those who cry.
    The ones who forgot how to smile.
For those who dream,
    Those who don't.
Run away from reality,
    Escape in your mind.

Masquerade

This is my masquerade,
 My harlequin dance.
This is my smile.
 My thorn wrapped face.
This is my dream,
 My silenced whispers.
This is my quartz mask,
 My carved tears.
This is the lump in my throat,
 My silent lies trickled out.
This is my beautiful lie,
 My perfect remake.
This is my masquerade,
 My harlequin dance.

Sky

I see scars
speckled across me,
like a midnight sky.

I tried,
to spread fake wings
and fly.

I fell back down,
like an Icarus,
doomed to the ground

Harmful Words

I have an armful
of harmful words.
With lies—like knives—
they hurt me.
I feel my fate was sealed
without a hint of pity.
Because I see such mystery,
unseen by the world.
Do you not see
the man in the corner?
How can that be when
he calls out to me.
I will just stay,
saying I'm fine,
With my armful
of harmful words.

Church Bells

The church bells ring
deep within my soul.
Calling like the dove,
that one faithful morn.

The organ's sweet songs,
beg for forgiveness,
singing His praise.
And I used to sing with it.

With my father as my pastor,
and my pastor as my kin.
I learned the ways of caring
the ways of His love.

But my church has forgotten
His ways of love.
They throw those in need
away like ripped cloth.

Like branches in a bonfire,
those poor people stand.
My church uses harsh words
to start the burning fires.

Because they are sinners,
is their only excuse.
Because they are sinners
Yet we are sinners too

With the church bells ringing
like a warning to all.
Crying out for those sinners,
Oh, sinners, come home.

Those Who Can't Count

Age does not matter to those
Who can't count,
those who find an age so high that the fear of death
consumes them.

Dollars do not matter to those
Who can't count,
those who find a number too low—with a fire of fear—the
dollar consumes them.

The past does not matter to those
Who can't count.
with wide eyed smiles, they'd listen to stories of old.

Time does not matter to those
Who can't count,
no fear consumes them, unlike those who count by seconds.

Nothing matters to those
Who can't count,
with only a fear of the dark in them.

What

What is
beautiful
about me

A Silence Answered

I shout to
the world—
Not even an echo answers me

No Fight

Who is wrong
And
Who is right
If there was never a fight
To be fought.

One-Sided

Why is it,
That love only exists
In a one-sided way

Sleep

I need
a type of sleep
That only love
can provide

My Body

Why is it
That I cannot love my body,
When you seem to love it so much.

For Someone Like You

I remember that day,
You told me
That my scars
Take away from my beauty.
I added more,
Because who would want
to be beautiful,
For someone like you.

A Hole in My Shoe

I have a hole
in my shoe.

        Like a hole
        in my heart.

It lets water in
Whenever it rains.

        It lets water in
        Whenever I cry.

Jealousy

That prick of jealousy,
Like that from
The spinning wheel,
Bites at my finger,
Stabbing my heart.

The threads of hatred
It spins,
Are like the hairs
On the head of a giant
Who stomps on those I love.

Like my pride,
Hurting my heart.

Debt

I am in debt.
I keep borrowing
Your love,
But never repaying it.

I keep taking
Your strength,
And using it.

I keep spending
Your mind,
And forgetting to pay the bill.

Stress

My hair falls
Away from my scalp,
Like leaves
From a tree in the fall.
Because Stress is no stranger to me.

Tragedy

I wanted to write our love story,
A tragedy
That never seems to end.
From the first touch
To the last smile.

You haunt my mind
Like you died years ago.
But isn't it you
I walk past on the streets?
Isn't it you
That I see with her,
Oh, so happy?

Great joy
Is in your new love.
I'm so happy for you.
At least,
I'll tell myself that.

Mind Games

Love is
Just a
Mind game
That no
One will
Ever win

Envy

Envy,
Is like a flower
That only blooms
When the sun
Turns away.

No Fight Left

I have
No fight
Left, in
This worthless
Body I
Call my
Own. This
Broken bone
Skeleton tries
To keep
Going. It
Will never
Succeed, for
I am
A broken
Hearted person.

The Floor

The floor seems
to swallow me,
On the day's
That I feel hollow.

The tile
And carpet
Chew at my mind.
Gnawing at the flesh of my brain.

The mosaics of the flooring
Chase me for miles.
Pulling itself from under my feet,
Making me fall to a grinding halt.

I just wish
The floor
Didn't have a death wish
For me.

Dear Flowers

Dear flowers,
That I picked when I was younger.

I'm sorry,
That I cut your life short.
Your beauty left me awestruck.
I wanted to hold you forever,
Not knowing you would die
If I plucked you from your home.
Not knowing you would rot
Even if I put you into water.

I wanted to show you off.
Giving you to friends and family.
Making you into crowns
I would throw away
at the end of the day.

I'm sorry,
But beautiful things
Always seem to die first.

Kindness

Being kind,
Makes no promises
of kindness retaliated.
People may still
Make it their aim,
To try and ruin you.
Because not all people
Are as kind as you.

Waiting

Loneliness bites at my heart,
The way the wolves
Chew at dead flesh.

Sadness slashes at my heart,
The way the great knights
Fought their enemies.

Anger shoots at my heart,
The way bullets do
In dueling fury.

Happiness sits in my mind,
Waiting, patiently, for a chance
To love my heart.

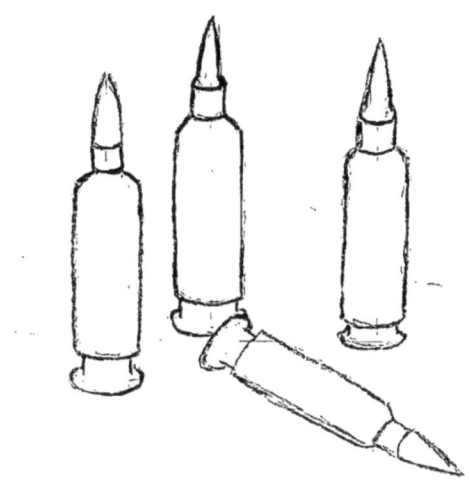

Volcano

Why is it,
That I
love you
With the passion
of a volcano,
But you barely
Love me,
With the passion
Of a stream?

Lies

Why did you lie,
And tell me that
The stab wound,
That you gave me,
Was nothing more
Than a tiny paper cut?

Were you not
Man enough,
To admit the pain
you caused?

Or were you too scared,
To take the death row,
From that throw,
Of the blade you hurt me with?

My Hair

My hair would never
Hold the curls I burnt into it.
They fell out,
Dropping to its usual straightness.
I hated that.

I wanted to be pretty,
like the curly haired girls.

I wanted to have hair,
That looked like the moon moved it,
Just like the oceans at night.

I wanted that hair,
Those beautiful curls.
Until the curls stayed.

I should have been happy,
With the beauty I had.

Ice

You stab me,
With a blade of ice.
It melts away,
Leaving no sign
Of the death you ordered me.

The only life
That drips away,
Is the life of the heart you killed.

The murder—
That you committed—
Still stains the shining snow
That was once my pale body.

And to think you call that love.

Why

Why your silence,
Hurts more
than a dull blade,
I will never know.

Why your voice,
Is like a siren's call,
Like nails on a chalkboard,
I will never know.

Why your look,
Causes the lowly caterpillars
in my stomach to fly,
I will never know.

Why your touch,
Burns my skin
Like an acid I beg for,
I will never know.

Why your kiss,
Feels like electricity
Shocking my body,
I will never know.

Why your love,
Is like a tornado,
Tearing and shredding my heart,
I will never know.

Why I love you,
The way you are:
The way you hurt
And break me,
I will never know.

Tears

The tears fall,
In time with the rain.
The rhythm of it
Hitting the floor,
Hitting the roof.
It matches.

The teardrops
Slide
Down
The leaf of my cheek.
The raindrops
Slide
Down.

The tears mix,
With the raindrops,
From the roof.

Statistic

I will never know,
The struggle of life.
The constant fighting with the world,
Just to prove I am something more than a statistic.

Winter

Winter

Winter is my one true love,
The chilled deathly feeling.
The smooth snowflakes,
Dancing like girls in movies.
The shining white ground,
The pain all around,
As you remember what once was.

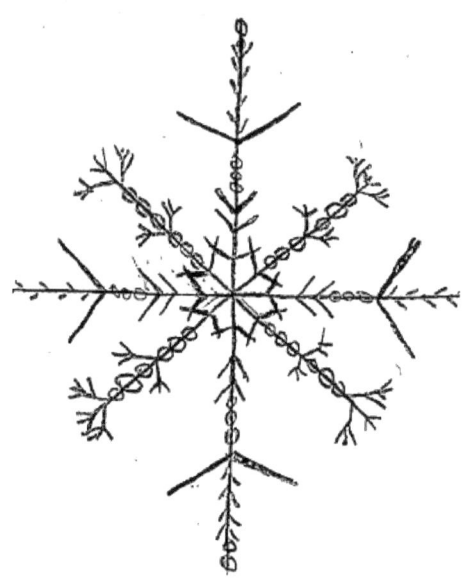

With Raspberry Tea

I take my medicine with
Raspberry Tea.
It's the only way I can.
The ten pills—like lies of getting better—choke me.
You have to get better; you say each day.
Like a threat, every day.
Like a bet, every day.
I wear a mask, every day,
Because I am better, I say,
With Raspberry Tea spilling out.

Wishing for More

The glass slid at her skin,
Leaving nothing but a thin white line.
She stared down at it.
Wishing for so much more.

Hurt

Her back hurts from carrying the world.
Her legs hurt from the miles she walked.
Her eyes hurt from the tears she has cried.
Her mind hurts from years of self-abuse.
Yet you still pulled her heart from her skin.

Staples

That painful smile you stapled,
It makes you bleed inside.
Through your heart and through your mind,
Like a waterfall,
It flows out

Him

That heart shattered look he gave you,
It was not weakness.
It was the heartlessness of your words.
It was your soulless eyes breaking him inside.

Bladed Tongue

My bladed tongue cut me as I spoke.
Your harsh whispers caused it.
To those who snickered behind me,
Those who snapped rude jokes.
I heard each word,
Crude and harmful.
But I bit my tongue,
Making myself bleed.

A Toast to Harsh Words

A toast to harsh words

To the star speckled skin it causes.
The whispers spilling out—just in earshot—
the tears cried at night.

To the heartbroken people,
The people who were shattered.
The people who can barely survive.

To the dead,
The ones to decide their death day
The ones to curse their birthday.

To the shattered,
The few to continue,
The few standing on sand with a rock in the distance.

A toast to harsh words,
The deadly criticisms,
and judgmental phrases.

A toast to harsh words
For ending innocent lives.

A Eulogy for My Heart and Mind

A eulogy for my heart and mind,
Dying together inside me.
They were loved for years,
Before they began to hurt.
They hurt themselves
In ways untold.
From shoveling bad memories
Out of their graves,
To lying to get nothing but attention.
They cut themselves from their home,
Walking miles without me.
They walked miles within me.
To think of how they once were:
Innocent,
Naive.
Such a change was uncalled for.
Now they lay,
Dead inside.
Dead before death claims them.
Forever and always,
This will be,
A eulogy for my heart and mind.

Toys

He never loved you,
If he looked to you without love dancing in his eyes.
You were his toy,
Something to break and throw aside.

Nothing

I am nothing to anyone,
Just a broken toy no one wants anymore.
Just a dead bouquet,
Given last Valentine's day.
I am nothing to anything.
Nothing to anyone.

A Love Letter to the Voices in My Head

A Love Letter to the Voices in My Head

I could not imagine my life without you.
You talked to me every day,
The only one who made the effort.
You spoke with such passion,
It was as if you loved,

tearing me down.
You probably did.
I lived with you for years,
Letting you shred my skin and soul.

You sold my heart,
For nothing but pennies.
You sold my mind,
For nickels and dimes.

I could not imagine life without you,
Until I had to.
It was strange to me,
The constant silence I began to live in.

It was like there was a gaping hole,
A bullet wound in a glass body.
I was used to you shattering me,
So much so I began shattering myself.

I miss you.
I miss the hatred you had for me,

When I had loved myself.
Now, no one loves me.

I tear myself up like you once had.
I miss the darkness you used to cover my pastels

My Voice

That voice I hear,
It's like a whisper of the devil.
He takes my voice and calls it against me,
For I could never say such foul things about anyone.
Anyone but me.

Snowflakes

The Snowflakes fall slowly,
Like the souls of those passed.
They twinkle like the eyes of my great grandmother,
The eyes that smiled as we sat.

The snowflakes fall slowly,
Like the idea I had of love.
It melts away as it touches me,
As though I were a fire.
As though I was unlovable.

The snowflakes fall slowly,
Like the friendships I once had.
Like the hugs I got from my friends,
That now curse my name.
As though I were made of flame.

Frostbite

I sit in a desperate silence,
A call for all to hear.
Begging to be saved,
From my frostbitten brain.

Here We Are

You said
you never would,
Yet
here we are now.

Cross

I wish I wore a cross those days.
Maybe it would have protected me.
Maybe it would have warned me of what was to happen.
Maybe I would have been safe.

If I had worn a cross those days,
Maybe it would have stopped sooner.
Maybe it would give me strength to speak up.

If I had worn a cross those days,
Maybe the tears would never fall.
Maybe those demons would have had to crawl away,
begging me to hide the beautiful gold cross around my neck.

Maybe it was my fault.

Maybe that gold cross would have burned my skin.
Maybe that cross would have made me cower in fear.

If I had just worn a cross those days.

Mean

Why are you
so nice to others
But
So mean
To yourself

Hate

I hate you.
I hate who you made me,
I hate what you left behind,
I hate how you treated me.
I hate you
Like I should have at the beginning*

*signed by what survived

If Size Mattered

It's funny,
How something so small,
Was like a sword through my soul.*

*if size mattered

Death

Maybe
Death
Doesn't
Even
Want
Me

Land and Sea

Why do you want the jungle between my legs
More
Than the ocean in my eyes

Sins

I used to like the way my skin burned
When I held my hand above a fire.
Like their sins melting off me

Day 1

Day 1: make up
It's a shame it made me feel
more beautiful than my own skin does.

Real Pain

The tears stain my eyes,
You have no right to cry
They whisper into my mind.
Why,
I cried,
Have I not suffered?

No
They snapped.
You will never know real pain*

*i know no real pain

Realization

The year you stop smiling,
You won't notice it.

The realization will come much later.

And it will hurt much more.

Blood

If tears were made of blood,
How many of us would still be alive*

*the tears we've all cried

Lines from a Shattered Soul

What's the harm in crushing broken pieces*

*lines from a shattered soul

Youth

I've had dreams.
About the books that I write.
The pride in the eyes of my family
As I sign a copy of
My liquid sunshine,
Poured from my heart.
But my midnight,
Mid-day,
Writing.
Will never be enough.
The world will never see me.
As anything but child.
My pains,
Are but jokes
Made by those who hurt me.
But I am young.
So, what pains have I really felt

Writing

I wish I could write out my heart.
Write out all the pain inside.
Write out that little demon called love,
And use my pen to end it.

I wish I could write out my tears.
Write out all that I've held back.
Write out the floods that live in my eyes,
And build little lakes with them.

I wish I could write out my pain.
Write out my bit lip.
Write out what I've felt,
And what I've lived through.

I wish I could write out my brain.
Write out our arguments.
Write out our battles: the good,
And my evil.

Lying

Pain is lying to yourself
In the fear that
you may learn to love yourself.

I Imagine

Why would people love me,
If I do not love myself.
If I try to end it all.

Like the red rain water from my wrist,
I imagine,
My tears running free.

Like the red waterfall from my neck,
I imagine,
I am running free.

Like the earthquake of my body,
I imagine,
I am shaking off this heavy skin.

Like the eclipse of my eyes,
I imagine,
I stop seeing my flaws.

Like the crack of thunder from my skull,
I imagine,
I feel no more pain.

Like the crushing of fallen rocks as my body falls,
I imagine,
I feel light and happy.

Like the rushing of water in my lungs,
I imagine,
I am breathing happily.

Like the filling floods in my body,
I imagine,
I am happy.
But what kind of happiness is that?

Crying Phone

Few know
How tears look
on a white screen.

Or see tears from a
Crying Phone

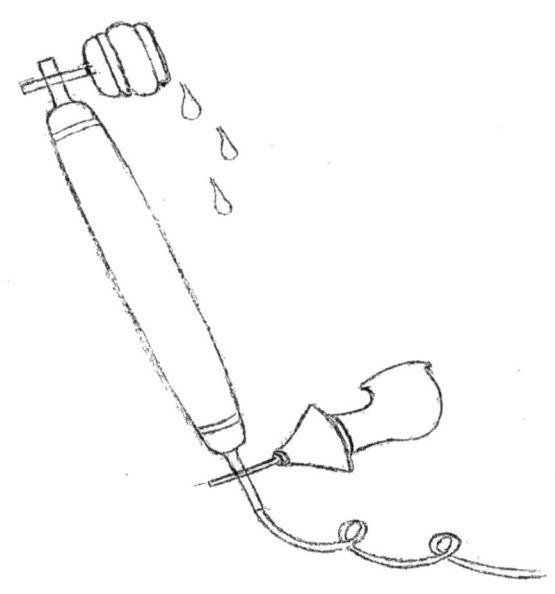

Pain and Love

Pain is love
Given by someone
who never loved you.

To a Broken Heart

What is love,
To a broken heart
Who knows only pain?

Action's Voice

Make the excuse one last time.
Tell me love,
Show me hate.

Tell me love,
Show me hate.*

*action's voice

Look at Me

Look at me.
See the sadness in my eyes.
The hurt in the once crystal oceans,
The storms that tore my pupil into pain.

Look at me

Unpaved

I always prayed
for my path.
with golden bricks paved,
to lead me home.
How immature is the thought?
Like a pathway of yellow bricks,
taking me to some distant land.
Like a parade
that gaily raves around me.
Absurd!
This worthless masquerade,
I call my own.
I wear it like a jacket in the cold.
With it,
my path will always be unpaved.

I Sit

How to feel in this heartbroken realm?
This painless music, cutting me at my wrists.
It fulfills my biggest dream.
It cancels out my heartbeat.
Letting it fade:
like the last scene of a terrible movie.

What can be said?
Not a word of confidence.
Not a smile spoken love claim.
Just the heart crushing tone of the one you once loved,
like the soft breeze in the start of summer.

With ~~these butterflies~~ these moths,
eating me inside,

I sit.
I sit.
Just because I can.

Away From Me

The butterflies in my stomach
escape through my eyes.

They want to fly free.
away from me,

like everything else

Insanity

Insanity is a safety
For those
Who have never felt sane.

Talking to the World

Will you ever end my suffering?
I whispered to the world.
Only you can end it,
She sighed in return

Relapse

After months of healed flesh,
Months of being clean:
I relapse every time.

The pain is like a drug—
I'm addicted.

The pain is like a drug—
I am addicted.

I'm addicted to the love of the pain
That I feel every day.
Emotional pain means nothing
To someone who loves the physical.
The new scars like new stars,
Speckling the summer's night sky.
My miracles
Being no more than a smile,
Hurt more than a blade ever will.
But I am addicted.

Inside and Out

Is pain all over
Better than
A deep pain inside

Still Love Me

I will never truly feel better
The way you want me to.
Please still love me.

Healing can Hurt

Healing can hurt
Like the knife that tried to end you.

Healing can hurt
Like his cold eyes as he walks away.

Healing can hurt
Like the needles you used to love.

Healing can hurt
Like gasping for air.

Healing can hurt
Like speaking of your past.

Healing can hurt
Like writing hurts too

My Mind

My scars do not define me,
They do not wear my clothes.
They are not gasping for air,
They are not crying,
They are not living,
They are not me.

One time,
Someone said that my scars
Are not battle wounds
That show I've survived,
But a show of weakness,
A show of attention seeking.
So I added more,
Sure that I would win my battled someday.

People stare at my scars,
Though now they are fading,
Questioning why I did it.
I simple say,
That they,
Have not lived a day in my mind.

Without You

What
Is
My
Life
Without
You

Push Me Down

I scraped my knee,
When I fell for you,
Falling down the steps
And onto the ground.
You helped me up
To push me down.
Why do I fall for you
Over and over,
When you push me down each time

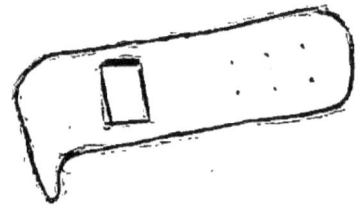

Music

Will my music ever be
Loud enough
To drown out your words?
Will the beat of the songs
Ever revive my heart?
Probably not.
Because I will always turn it off
Just to hear you talk.

Attachment

Why is it
I get so attached
To so many people,

When
no one ever
gets attached to me.

My Dear

My dear,
You paint beautifully,
The scars on my body
Are the only proof.
But I know,
You could paint the sky,
Better than the Master
Himself

With the Effort of Moving

My body creaks
With the effort of moving.
I am not old.
Just abused.
I have mutilated my body.
Ignored it's pleads
To be cared for.
My body creaks
With the effort of moving.

Letters

To the people
Who never wrote to me:
Thank you for your words.
That kind silence,
Stuck in the air,
As I wait for your letter to appear.

It won't come.
I don't expect it to.
But I like to imagine
Paper,
With your scent,
And smooth ink
Written by your hand.

Much like how you write on my skin,
Your fake words of love.
How come,
You use me as paper,
When I ask for the letter?

Am I the note for someone else?

Violence

Put a knife to my neck,
To show me you love me.
Because violence
Is the only way
You show affection

Cyanide

I must admit.
Having a
Taste for
Someone like you,
Is more toxic,
Than a taste
For cyanide.

Denial

Why am I so hurt,
That you moved on,
After I denied you?

Repeat

What truth
Is there
In what your mind
Says on repeat?

An Angel's Kiss

You make the thorn
You put in my thumb
Feel like
A kiss from an angel

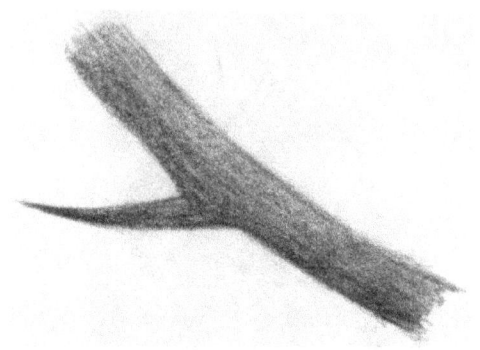

Pain that Loves Me

What's wrong with
The love
I used to love.
And the pain
That used to hurt me.

How Could You

I cough out my heart,
The blood drips off my lips.
My mind cries out
In an unknown pain.
How could you do this,
My heart howls
From at my knees,
As I kneel to it.
How could you hurt me,
It fumes
As I lift it from the floor.
How could you hurt me,
I whisper
In a soft sadness.
How could you hurt me.
I place it back in.

The Silent Blade

Silence is
As deadly as a blade.
Both slice at the throat
of their victims.
Taking their words
From their mouths.
Taking their spirits
From their bodies.
The only difference,
Is silence leaves no evidence.

Birds

I am envious
Of the
free flying birds.

The way their wings
Help them soar.

They can fly away,
As far as they can,
And fly back when they want to.

Their home is the sky—
The stars,
Their closest friend.

Why can't I just fly away?

A Kiss

What harm,
Can one kiss do,
When he holds the blade
Against my throat

Love Scar

The kiss
You put on my neck,
Is more of a scar,
Than a love mark.

Lost

I lost my face,
When I lost
my smile.
The day that
the first pain started.

I lost my face,
When I lost
My tears.
The day that
The faucet ran dry.

I lost my face,
When I lost
My will.
I fought back,
But in the end
The darkness won again.

Anxiety

I always loved
The way anxiety felt.
The heart stopping feeling,
Making me guess
If my heart was
Beating too fast,
Or not at all

Dead Butterflies

My stomach turns
At the thought
of you touching me,
now.

Used to,
My stomach fluttered,
As though butterflies
Inhabited it.

Why would you kill
My beautiful butterflies?

Rope

You knot
My intestines,
Like they are only rope.
You use them
to climb to my heart,
Even though
You know it's locked.

Much Too Well

I've begged my eyes
To stop crying,
for just one day.

To be the well,
That ran dry.

To be the faucet,
that was turned off.

They listened,
Much too well.

Compliments

I tried to compliment,
The person who stares back.
The blue eyed,
Brown haired,
Woman across from me.

She refused the compliments,
Saying she deserved none.

My Foe

Silence,

He is my foe,
An enemy I have yet to beat.

He bashes at me
With snarled,
Bare teeth.

He thrusts at me,
With knives
And arrows,
Thrown from far away.

He yells at me,
In fury,
In a sound
That will never be heard,
But I feel it in me.

He tries to win.
In a way that is unhealthy.
He tries to win,
Just to say he beat me.

His eyes are sad,
They are worn away
By the tears he has cried.

His body is hollow,
Clear as glass.

Silence is broken.

The Moon

My eyes would tire,
After a Midnight's read.

The moon shone down,
Trying to imitate the sun.

The stars twinkled,
As though they wished
To fall fluidly,
Like the water in a warm shower.

My eyes blinked heavily.
A yawn escaped the pink of my lips.

I was tired.
Exhausted.

I was tired:
Of yelling in families.
Tears in public.
Harsh whispers from behind.
Slow movements.
Trying to walk on.

Of heavy feet.
Dull eyes.
Greasy hair.
Shaking hands.
Fake smiles gracing dead faces.

But the moon,
She saw.
She saw the tears I hid,
In silent sobbing at midnight.

The moon,
She saw the broken hearts

Of the lost.

She heard.
She listened:
To the quiet prayers.
The whispered screams.

The longing for a happy life.

The moon.
She knew.

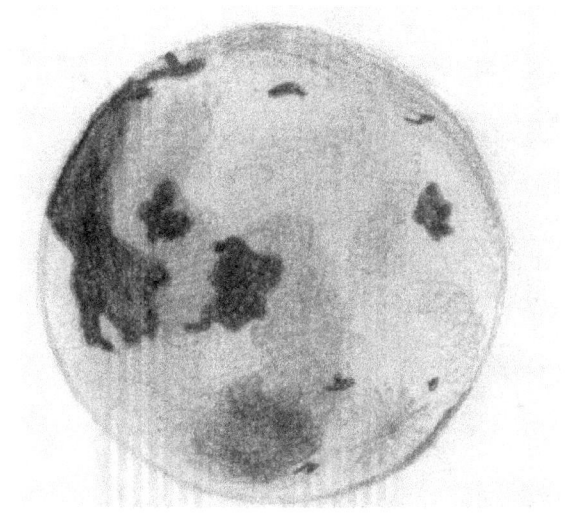

Sharp Blade

When the blade
Is sharp,
It's supposed
to hurt less.
You've taught me,
That's a lie.

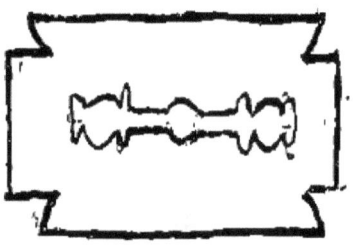

Death Doesn't Seem

Death doesn't seem
So scary,
When your hand is on my throat.

Death doesn't seem
So scary,
When your lips are on mine.

Death seems terrifying,
When I watch your feet as you
Walk away.

A Stabbing

My toes curled.
My eyes shut tight.
My breath sped.
The world seemed so distant.

When did a stab wound,
Start to feel like an orgasm.

Before or After

Does pain
Hurt worse
After you
Acknowledge
It?
Or before you
Knew you could
Live it.

Spring

Spring

Spring is beautiful,
Unlike me.
The warmth and coolness
Of the season seems to contradict itself.
Much like glorious fall,
With more growth than death.
With more life.
I enjoy the spring,
Showing off,
In her bright colors.

I Dream in Bright Colors

I dream in bright colors,
Pretty pastels.
These hues of my childhood—
The hues of my life.
I see each color,
Deep within,
Like a lost secret
Underneath my skin.

Raspberry

Sweet
People are
Hard to find;
Like finding a
Raspberry
In a
Strawberry
field.

Lavender

The sweet scent,
the feeling of calm and comfort.
The kind color,
the lace on the sleeves of that dress I once loved.
The warm taste,
the way those cookies melted on my tongue.
The relief,
the feeling I always want.

Fire

May the fire in your words
Never be extinguished.
And May the forest of your soul
Never ignite.

Incomplete

I believe nothing should be left incomplete.
Whether it be book, song, or drawing.
More importantly, no person should be left incomplete.
Give them back their heart.

Your Worth

Never let someone make you ponder of your worth.
You are worth more than the gold on Earth.
You are worth more than the diamonds in the mines.
You are worth more than the stars in the sky.
You are worth more than anything.
Remember that.

Love

Shiny things and diamond rings
mean nothing to someone who truly loves.
The most beautiful thing is the other's smile.

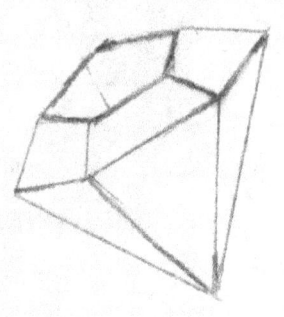

You First

Don't let them touch you the way you don't want.
Put yourself first.
They will not make you happy,
Only you can.
Don't let them be the bad guy of your story,
You don't need a prince in shining armor to protect you.
You are strong,
You can fight.

Scientist

Playing with her ring,
She bit at her lip.
Her eyes darted around.
They made her that way.
But,
She was recreating herself.
She was no perfect made creature,
She was her own scientist.

Holey

There's a hole in me.

I took out my stomach,
Because beautiful people are thin.

I took out my heart,
Because beautiful people are not emotional

I took out my brain,
Because beautiful people don't get depressed.

I took out my eyes,
Because beautiful people don't cry.

I took out my lungs,
Because beautiful people don't breathe heavy.

I took out my voice box,
Because beautiful people don't talk back.

The truth is,
Beautiful people are everywhere.
We are beautiful.

If You Love

If you love,
Do not lose
Yourself.
They do not rule you.
They do not own you.
You are still free.
You are no caged bird,
But a soaring eagle.

Musical Dreams

Let my broken melody,
Be completed.
Let this unsteady tempo slow,
To a calm heartbeat.
Let this loud crashing of cymbals
Fall into the soft whispers of beautiful flutes.
Let this nightmare,
Drift into a sweet dream for me to remember tomorrow.

I Dream

I dream,
like a reality I want to relive every night,
the same dreams on repeat.
The dreams of love, happiness, success.

Just dreams,
they seem so far away.
Like the stars,
drifting above me,
All knowing,

Seeing my future play out.
Seeing what is in store for me.
Seeing me grow into what I've always wanted to be.
Seeing my love, happiness, success.

I Can Write Out My Own Future

I can write my own happy endings.

If I can write people into existence,
Love stories from thin air,
Fairytales from a forest scene,
Passion from a warm flame inside,
Animals from the tears in my eyes,
Poems from my hurt,
Stories from my crazy mind.

I can write my own happy endings.
I will.*

*i can write out my future

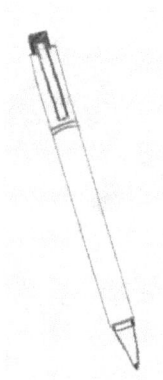

Fake Smiles

My heart cried as I smiled at him.
Fake smiles are my specialty,
I make them in Baker's dozens.
He looked away.
The poor boy,
He must regret not keeping it in his pants.
We passed by,
Never meeting his sad eyes.
He must learn to hide those eyes.
He's as easy to read as an open book.
I keep a ripped bookmark in him,
Like a cut in his soul,
As he left his favorite in me.

Your Eyes

I would love to be lost
In the dusk fallen forest
People mistake for your eyes

Snow

You are beautiful without makeup,
It is like the mountains
Begging for snow
Just to mask its perfect beauty

Let Her Grow

Why pick a rose
When you want to admire her.*

*let her grow

Cardinal

You are still
In every
Cardinal
I have ever seen.

In every
Butterfly,
You flutter by
Kissing my cheek.

In every
Bright eyed child
—excited for the future—
Staring at me in loving awe.

In every second,
Smiling down to me.
I know you're there,
Always protecting me

Questions

I'm not sure
of my place in this world,
Nor will I ever be.
It will be like the rainbow,
Asking its purpose.
Or a butterfly,
Pondering,
why
his life is so short.
Like the rain cloud,
Wondering why people hate her.
Or the sunshine,
Thinking people love her.
I will never know
My place in this world,
And I will question every second of life.

Sunshine

I couldn't write to save my life,
When I was in my darkest place.
When I was in that cold dark pit.

Maybe the warmth
of my newfound sunshine
Will rescue me.

Cats

A black cat in my lap,
purring as I stroked him,
His eyes like wisdom,
His body, stone.
He looked at me and meowed sweetly,
telling me his goodbye.

So now I sit,
a grey cat in my lap,
purring as I stroke her.

A Beautiful Mind

A beautiful mind,
is like Life within Death.
Spring within Harvest.
Beauty within Disgust.
You think
of your fate,
letting fear consume you.
Control your fears,
Beautiful Mind,
And live within yourself.

Words

Don't underestimate
the power of words.

The voice can shatter glass.
It can crumble stone.

The pen can kill.
It can be a sword through a helpless soul.

The vocabulary can build worlds.
It can create love.

The word can bring life.
It can call out love to an unforgiving world.

Addiction

Like a drug—
I am addicted to him.

Like those pills
For that high—
I kiss him.

Like the smoking
For that calm—
I hold him.

I think of him,
Constantly.
He lives in my brain,
Walking through it like he owns me.
He owns me.
I am his.
But what am I to him.
Other than a drink,
That he claims
He can quit anytime

He is drunk,
On me.
Like I am a flavored rum
That he mixes in his life.
He drinks from a small cup,
Consuming my unused body.
He loves it.
He loves the burn in his throat
As he drinks me.

How curious it is,
How we push each other away,
Though it is like we cannot live
Without the other.

One day,
I hope to be his water,
And he, my air.
Healthy love,
Where we may love,
And be loved in turn.

He is my air,
The drug I need to live.

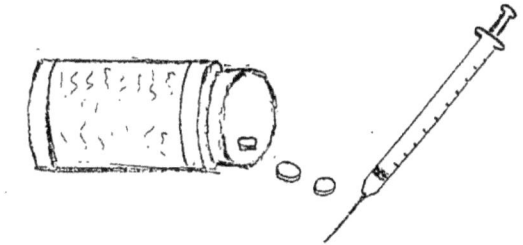

Fear of Growth

Fear of growth
Is fear of life.

Fear of growth
Is fear of love.

Fear of growth
Is fear of knowledge.

Have no fear.

A flower only blooms if it grows.

My Heart

My heart quivers
at the thought of you
Touching me

If My Scars Could Talk

If my scars could talk,
They would tell me I am healing.
They would whisper sadly,
Of their existence
Because,
I am too beautiful
To hurt myself.

Roughly

Treat me roughly.
Hard enough to distract me from real pain.

Treat me gently.
Soft enough to distract me from real pain.

Treat me with love
Kind enough to distract me from real pain.

Treat me like I'm important.
Important enough to feel no real pain.

Pastels

I wish the pastels
Of the world
Could take over my life.

The soft pinks,
And blue,
And lavender,
And yellow:
All like kind glances.
They may not remove the darkness,
But they can soften it.

That's all I need,
A softened darkness.
A kind voice to speak to me,
Through all the yelling,
Deep in my mind.

To make the shadowy figures chasing me
Into sweet butterflies
To flutter past
On a cool spring day.

A beautiful sunrise
On the endless night
I used to
Only survive in.

Like the little flowers
That grow in the spring,
In pastel shades,
I wish to grow.
I want to be beautiful like them.
I want to be tall and strong,
Even if I am growing through a sidewalk.

Like a new lamb,

White and petite,
I want to be loved,
And cared for.
Having my wool stroked,
Being precious.

Like a rainbow,
I want to be stared at in awe.
My sweet colors after the storm.
I want to be looked at,
And be smiled to,
Because I mean the end of something bad.
I mean the beginning of light
In their lives.

I want the pastels of this world
To become me,
So I may be looked upon
With love.

My Writing

Can I really write
Like my heart dreams I can?
Or am I a lost cause,
Dreaming of a Promised Land
That I will never be
Welcomed into?
I hope,
The gates will open
That I may pass through,
And sit with great authors
All better than I
Could ever be.

Forest of My Scalp

I grow my hair out,
Like the forest grows her trees.
They make her more beautiful.
Maybe I
May mirror her beauty.

My Little Flower

The flowers
Show their face
In a shy magnificence.
Much like you do.

Its petals hide the center,
Like you hide behind
Your hands.

It's stem
is tall and strong,
Much like you are.

My Little flower,
Keep growing.

Currency of Love

We paid each other,
In the currency of love.
The coins,
made from kisses,
The dollars,
made from touch.
And
We were always rich.

Loving Myself

I will only
Love myself,
If anyone
ever proves
That I am worth it.

Your Kiss

The weak feeling
In my legs,
Caused by your kiss,
Makes the hair on my arms lift.
If I could keep this feeling forever,
Our lips would never separate.

The Difference

You were different.
There were no chills.
No heart stopping touches.
But, our love was pure.
It was less butterflies,
And more flowers.
It was comfortable,
Like no other love had been.
It was comfortable,
Like I had lived many lives with you.
It was comfortable,
Like we had never loved before

Do Flowers Bloom?

Flowers in
The sunshine
Often bloom.

Flowers in
The dark
Never do.

What's Wrong With Loving You?

What's wrong with loving you?

Loving the way you smile shyly
As I tell you you're beautiful.
You've never
Been complimented enough.

Loving the parts you hate,
Even when you say you see
No beauty in them.
They're perfect.

Loving your mind,
Even though you say
You will never be as smart as me.
I don't believe you.

Loving your hand,
Because it has dried my tears
More times
Than mine have.

Loving your hair,
Even though you hate it,
You still let me
Play with it.

Loving your emotions,
Just because you don't understand them.
No one does,
But that never mattered to me.

Loving you
even though
You will never
be loving me.

The Meadow

Let me run
my hands
Through the meadow
Of your hair
As our
Lips
Meet once again

Do I Know Love?

I write about a love
That I have never experienced.
But my mind is wild enough
To have lived it
A thousand times over.

Whoever You Want

Loving the lilies
Like the dandelions
And clovers,
Just proves
You can love whoever you want to.

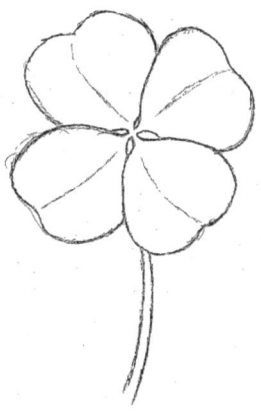

Beautiful

What better way
To spend a rainy afternoon,
Than to lie with you by
My side,
Your torso,
Moving ever so slightly,
In rhythm with your breath.
You look beautiful
In this hibernation.
But you always look beautiful.

I'm Hungry for You

My stomach growls
In an ever growing hunger
for you.
Like a wild wolf,
You seemed to tame.
Like an angry bear,
You seemed to calm.
Like a hungry body,
You fed love.*

*im hungry for you

I Only Have Horns

My dear,
You were an angel,
But I failed
To see those magnificent
Wings that let you hover.
I liked to pretend,
That maybe I was the one,
With wings.*

*i only have horns

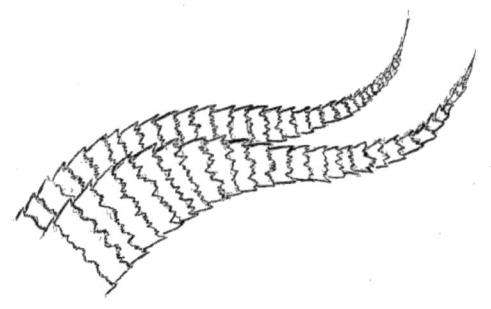

The Rain

The rain trickling
From the heavens,
The clouds heavy with
An unknown sorrow.
This is a perfect day
To read poems to them,
And maybe take their pain away.

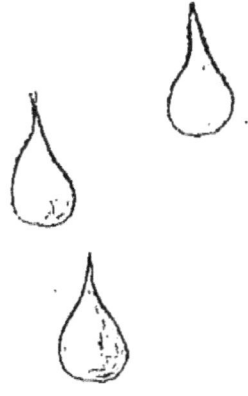

Sharp Edges

The world
Isn't so bad,
If you blur
the sharp edges.

Do You Love Me?

When the midnight
Becomes mid-day.
When the clouds
Hide the shining sun.
When the birds stop
Their sweet bird songs.
Even when
I try to sing along.

Meet me there,
Beneath the lightning struck trees.
Kiss me gently
Like I am unique.
Hold me tightly
So I may never leave.
Just tell me that
You love me.

Moon Lover

Moon lover,
Stare up in awe.
Stare into the shining
Night sky,

Just to get a taste,
Of the moon
and her endless love.

To get a taste of
What time she has seen.

To get a taste of
What tides she has moved,
The oceans she manipulated
Throughout her time of life.

Moon lover,
Love to your dying days.

Her Smile

Her smile,
Oh, the beauty in it.
Yet she sees nothing.
For the moon cannot
see her own shining,
Just its effect on the world.

What if I Were the Moon?

What if I,
were the moon?
Would I reflect the sun's
Purest beauty,
Or hide my face from her,
In the shiest manner?

What if I,
Were the clouds?
Would I float by,
Happy in the
oceans of my sky?

What if I,
Were the stars?
Would I flicker,
Watching the world below me,
As they stare back in awe?

What if I,
Were the rain?
Something so hated,
Something so loved?
The life that is provided
And stolen away.

What if I,
Were the thunder?
I could shake houses,
Just by speaking.
I could scream my name,
Just to prove that I was coming.

What if I,
Were the lightning,
Lighting the world?
If I could pronounce

Myself with the light,
I could be proud.

What if I,
Were the sky itself?
The blue above?
The Heavens looking down
On the lesser of man?

Such a dream it is.

Potholes

Bad things
Should be a pothole,
Not the cliff
It may feel like it is.

Butterfly

A major transition,
Is always needed
If you want to learn to fly.
Because a caterpillar
Must become a butterfly.

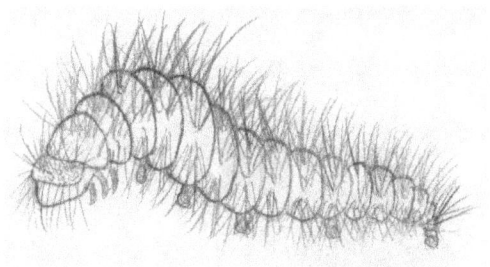

I Love Me

Will there ever
Be a day,
That I will look in the mirror,
And smile
—A smile people claim to love—
Just because,
I love me.

Summer

Summer

The summer
is my least favorite season,
The bright lights,
The heat formed by
a Greater Being.
But I love summer nights,
When the stars shine at their brightest,
Almost calling to me like a siren.
Calling to me,
Come home

We Are All People

Sweet girl,
Never compare yourself to another.
You've endured enough pain for a thousand men,
So have they.
They are not better,
Nor are you.
We are all people.
That's all that should matter.

Everyway

You are beautiful
in every way,
dearest,
Never believe
you aren't enough.

Dear Girl

Dear girl,
You are beautiful.
The way you smile,
The way you laugh,
The way your eyes grin
when you are happy.
The music in your heart,
The lyrics in your soul.
Beautiful girl,
Keep singing.

My Home

The stage is my home,
The music,
my magic.
The loud clapping,
Like a joy in my heart.
It will never be a job,
For I love it too much.

Country Summers

Summer days,
Summer nights,
When the warm air hits you.
Those deep breaths of fresh country air,
Always seems to surround you.
Being far from City lights,
Watching the stars sounder by.
Such a relaxing thought.
The branches wave,
With fresh leaf hands,
As though to send a greeting.
The grass soft and plush,
Bouncing as I walk.
The country summers and city falls
Always seems to be in me.
With season hearts and happy thoughts,
I wish to live here forever.

Precious Child

Precious child,
What would the world be without you?
Without your smile, the sun would shine dull.
Without your eyes, the stars would only hide.
Without your being, the world would halt.

Precious child,
What would my world be without you?
Without your words, I could not smile.
Without your touch, I would not continue.
Without your soul, I would not wish to live.

Tap Your Foot

Tap your foot to the beating of your heart.
Use the steady sound as a base for the music of your life.
The song of your breath.
The words of your mind.
The rhythm of your footsteps.
Tap your foot,
Tap your foot to your music

Opal

The gem of her heart became cracked.
No amount of polishing would fix it.
But she was still shining.
Like a flaw in an opal,
It only made her more beautiful.

Late Night Writing

My late-night writing,
Was—and is—better
than any therapy session.
Like talking to the stars,
Screaming my problems to the moon.
Whispering my tears to the night foxes.
Spilling out my heartbreak to the shadowed rooms.
Smiling through my tears with the wolves.
Laughing with the lightning bugs.
Dancing with the moths.
Leaping with the pillows from my bed.
Twirling with the sheets.
Opening my eyes hours later,
With new writing,
Written by the night sky.

The Dark

I'm still afraid of the dark.
The things that haunted me in shadows for years,
They made me scared of what is watching me.

But I have a night light,
It flickers in the dark.

It is beautiful,
A glowing wonder,
My protection,
My safety.

Something I know will always be there

Midnight

With heavy eye lids,
I write at midnight.
Ideas filter out of my mind,
Like water through cheese cloth.
Who ever said writing was easy.

Ode to the Voice

Ode to the voice—silent in the night.
To the bladed words that answer.
The knife engraved with a deadly *shut up.*
The bullets screaming *no one cares.*

Ode to the voice—whispering in the night.
To the warm blanket of its words.
The dull scent of blood on its breath.
The shaky voices strengthens.

Ode to the voice—talking in the night.
To the new found confidence like a fragile glass shield.
The new thorns to cradle it.
The small cracks slowly filled.

Ode to the voice—yelling in the night.
To the small sound—a new symphony!
The strong clap of thunder.
The loud crack of a falling wall.

Ode to the voices—ruling the night.
To the tiny ants who scream together.
The few made many.
We rule the world!

Touch A Star

If I could,
but touch a star,
and eat the Milky Way
like a candy bar.
To hug the planets,
like teddy bears and
kiss an asteroid,
in loving care.
To float away
and touch the sky.
That's my wish until I die.

Colorblind

We live in a world
of black and white.
A lonely life curled
in this one-sided sight.

We cry at what we see.
This bland world
consumes us.
Its dullness rules.

Like a fate of a blade,
it thrusts at us.
Like a gun,
it screams.

It was fun,
wasn't it?
When we were young
and saw in color.

Some will promise change,
a change in ways,
in the hues of sight,
but they lie.

We live in a world
of black and white.
A lonely life curled
in this one-sided sight.

But with my fight
You will find,
Not everyone
Is Colorblind.

What is Beautiful

What is beautiful,
To a person who sees
No beauty in themselves—
Is it the way the sun
reflects in the pools of your eyes,
Or the moonlight
Making your face glow in perfection.
The stars sparkling
Like your smile.
The way the wind
Reminds them of your beautiful laughter.
You make the sun jealous, my dear,
The moon,
envious of your light.
The stars are embarrassed
To try and shine with you.
The wind angered that
Your laughter is purer.
You are so beautiful.

I Don't Care

I don't care
If people belittle me
For my problems
That they can't see.

You

Your shining smile takes my breath away. Your kind eyes are like life to me. Your gentle touch is like warming myself by a fire. Your soft hair is like the grass in spring as I stretch in a meadow. Your kisses are like that of an angel. You hold me as I cry. You stroke my hair like no one ever has. You make me feel human. And you have the audacity to ask why I love you.

Love

If my heart beats fast
For you,
Is it racing
Because you love me,
Or because I love you?

Skeleton

Your skeleton
Must be as beautiful
As your body is
On the outside

The Heart Ring

My father
Gave me a ring,
To make me feel loved.
It had a heart
Made from the jewels of his own.
And the band as silver and shining
As his mind.
My father is as beautiful
As the ring on my hand.

Your Affection

I am overwhelmed,
By the force of your affection,
It reminds me
That I can be loved
By even myself.

Showers

I hate showers,
Until I step in them.
The steam from the warmth,
The soothing patter on my back.
Like the rain,
Trickling off the roof of my house,
The water drips from
My body,
Slides away from my hair.
My breath calms,
The world disappears

A Poem

A poem is a life
Being born from the mind.
Being birthed by pains.
Growing from a need
To feel complete.
Living because someone,
Somewhere,
Needed to feel whole again.
Thriving because
Who wrote it
Put their life into it.

To the Reader

To the reader
Who never learned to read.
To the writer
Who never learned their words.
To the artist
Who never learned the colors.
To the musician
Who never learned notes.
To the magician
Who never learned tricks.
Keep trying,
You're almost there.

Sweet

The caramel
Kissed my tongue
As I let it rest there.
The sweet taste unraveled,
Like thread
Leaving its spool.

The quiet of the room
Encased me,
Like I was a butterfly—
Unborn—
In the silence my cocoon.

The dull light
Shone down,
Like the sun was
Dying at noon.

Be True

Be true
To who you are,
Not who you want to be.

Painting

My friend would paint
The most beautiful pictures.
But she was too shy to admit that.

Her skills challenged
That of masters.
But she was too shy to admit that.

Her beautiful paintings
Should be in museums,
But she was too shy to admit that.

My dearest friend,
She was so beautiful,
But she was too shy to admit that.

I am a Woman

You think,
That I,
am a doll.
That I,
am a poseable figure.
A dainty porcelain body,
With a pretty painted face?

You think,
That I,
am a toy?
A man-made thing,
Created for
your nasty hands
To play with?
Something that you can break,
And throw away?

Oh,
How wrong you are.

I,
am a goddess.
A heaven-sent being.
A perfectly built form,
Made to please
No one but me.
And With the beauty of the clouds,
How could I not be?

I,
am a queen,
Pure royalty
At its finest.
My crown—of gold and diamond—
Sets on the head of my breasts.
I hold my head high,

Because my enemies,
They will never see me cry.
I am too strong for that.

I,
am an angel.
My wings spread
From the dip in my back.
My halo is held up,
By bad memories
Of people
Ripping my feathers out.
But I can still fly,
Because I am better than they
Could ever try to be.

I,
am Mother Earth.
I can grow a forest,
From between my legs.
I can cry seas
Into existence,
Through tears that only I let fall.
I can make life,
Bring humanity into existence,
Through wide hips
That rise and fall,
Like the beautiful canyons
That grace the earth.

I,
am a weeping willow.
Crying for my kind.
Sobbing for those
That the evil of man cut down.
Silently praying,
That I could survive,
To see another sunrise.
Seeing the stars rise and set with me.

I,
am the sun.
The shining light
That blinds you,
If you stare to long.
The glowing orb
That warms you.
That radiant heat,
That shapes you into life.

I,
am the definition,
Of beauty.
Like every other woman is.
We are blooming like roses:
Beautiful, soft petals
with sharp, ready Thorns.
We are geodes:
Rough and strong,
But shining with gemstones,
Deep within our skin.

I am not a doll.
I, am a woman.

I am not a toy.
I, am a woman.

I am the world.

The Sky

The sky,
Like a butterfly:
Flutters past,
In this fast,
Day to day pace.
Like the race
Of life.
With a knife,
To cut the clouds as they go by.
With the sky,
As a pretty butterfly

Who I Am

Who are you?
You ask in a terrified tone.

Who am I?

Who I am,
Can never be described,
By words alone.
Because I am so
Much more,
Than any word has ever been.

Commander

The moon light,
Can cast shadows
Across the unknown lands.
The seas do
Only it's bidding.
The oceans only bow to it.
The star struck lovers,
Hold hands beneath its
shining love.

I am the moon light,
True Commander
of the seas.
The oceans bow
Only down to me.
I see the lost lands
That no one inhabits.
I light the world,
For lovers to hide in.
Until the morning light
comes to find me.

The Cup

Raspberry Tea
is always in season,
but only when the world
changes with the cups.

www.ingramcontent.com/pod-product-compliance
Lightning Source LLC
Chambersburg PA
CBHW072150100526
44589CB00015B/2164